STONEHENGE

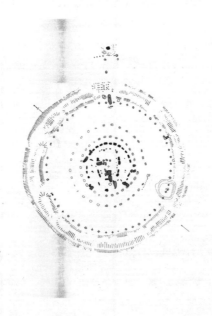

Originally published in Wales by Wooden Books Ltd. in 2001; first published in the United States of America in 2002 by Walker Publishing Company, Inc.

Published simultaneously in Canada by Fitzhenry and Whiteside, Markham, Ontario L3R 4T8

For information about permission to reproduce selections from this book, write to Permissions, Walker & Company, 435 Hudson Street, New York, New York 10014

Printed on recycled paper.

Illustration on the half title page: The 1973 Thom survey of Stonehenge.

Library of Congress Cataloging-in-Publication Data

Heath, Robin (Robin F.)
    Stonehenge / by Robin Heath.
        p.   cm.
    Originally published: Presteigne, Powys, Wales : Wooden Books, 2001.
    Includes bibliographical references.
    ISBN 0-8027-1385-8 (alk. paper)
    1. Stonehenge (England)   2. Megalithic monuments—England—Wiltshire.   3. Prehistoric peoples—England—Wiltshire.   4. Wiltshire (England)—Antiquities.   I. Title. ·
DA142 .H43   2002
936.2′319—dc21   2001056787

Visit Walker & Company's Web site at www.walkerbooks.com

Printed in the United States of America

2 4 6 8 10 9 7 5 3

STONEHENGE

STONHING

Robin Heath

WOODEN
BOOKS

Walker & Company
New York

To Rebecca, Matthew, and Lea

Pictures have been taken from a wide selection of rare antiquarian books and most of them are credited where they appear. The engravings on page 3 are from Inigo Jones's book of 1655, the engraving on page 24 is from William Stukeley, 1740, the lower picture on page 31 is from Walpoole's late eighteenth-century Modern British Traveller, *and the illustration on page 54 is from Alexander Thom, courtesy of Eoghan MacColl. Other illustrations are by the author.*

An early drawing of Stonehenge, from Lucas De Herre, 1569.

CONTENTS

Introduction	1
Digging in the Dark	4
The Stonehenge Landscape	6
Travels to the Otherworld	8
Stonehenge Culture	10
Barrowloads of Gold	12
Astronomy and Geometry	14
The First Stonehenge	16
Aubrey Holes and Station Stones	18
Sarsens and Trilithons	20
Woodwork in Stone	22
Erecting the Stones	24
The Modern Picture	26
The Ghost in the Machine	28
Here Comes the Sun	30
Woodhenge	32
Calendar Capers	34
Alternative Stonehenge	36
The Lunation Triangle	38
Predicting Eclipses	40
Stonehenge Complete	42
Rolling Stones	44
The Middle Ground	46
Sacred Geometry	48
Surveying the Circle	50
Stonehenge Dwarfed	52
Star Culture	54
Inspirational Stonehenge	56
Further Reading	58

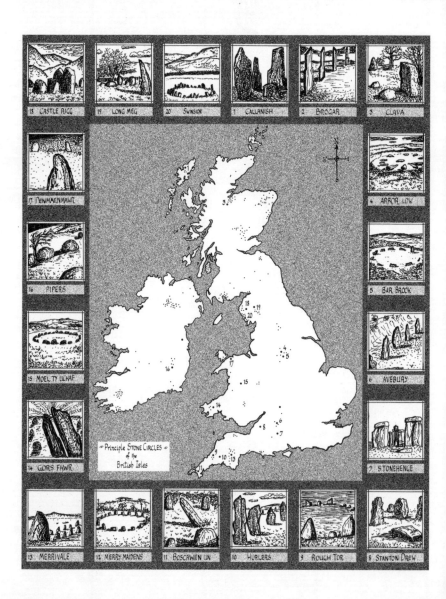

18. CASTLE RIGG 19. LONG MEG 20. SWINSIDE 1. CALLANISH 2. BROGAR 3. CLAVA

17. PENMAENMAWR 4. ARBOR LOW 16. PIPERS 5. BAR BROOK 15. MOEL TY UCHAF 6. AVEBURY 14. GORS FAWR 7. STONEHENGE

Principle STONE CIRCLES of the British Isles

13. MERRIVALE 12. MERRY MAIDENS 11. BOSCAWEN UN 10. HURLERS 9. ROUGH TOR 8. STANTON DREW

INTRODUCTION

Stonehenge is Britain's national temple. Attracting almost one million visitors a year, the monument has become the country's most visited tourist attraction, now a World Heritage site. Yet despite its popularity, this prehistoric monument remains shrouded in mystery and still provokes many questions in both layman and specialist alike—who built it, when, and for what purposes? Why were all those huge stones moved such unfeasibly long distances and then placed so precisely?

These questions remained largely unanswered until fairly recently, and this book charts the emergence of Stonehenge into the collective modern psyche, from naive medieval speculations through modern scientific methodology and New Age revelations.

When accurate techniques of radiocarbon dating became available in the late 1960s, the dating for the original monument was pushed back over a thousand years, to before 3000 B.C. This left an embarrassing split in the archaeological record, the construction of Stonehenge being initiated before the Great Pyramid and almost every other megalithic building in the ancient world (*megalith* is Greek for "large stone"). The previously held idea that civilization and culture had gradually diffused from the Middle East became untenable. An apparently safe archaeological paradigm, *diffusionism*, collapsed.

Interestingly, at precisely this same time, the astronomy, metrology, and geometry of Stonehenge and many other stone circles was being revealed, not always with the blessing or agreement of orthodox archaeologists. A lively ferment of debate between archaeologists and astronomers, historians and engineers in the early 1970s initiated a most creative period of reassessment for Stonehenge and its original purpose.

Stonehenge is far more than just an impressive display of huge stones. If it were merely that, it would fail to maintain such a powerful presence within our present culture. Up to forty thousand people arrive each year in the hope of observing the midsummer sunrise from the monument. Stonehenge is a symbol or icon of *Albion*, the ancient wisdom of Britain and of different cultural values from a vanished time. Using Stonehenge as a lens, we can truly see into the mind of a Neolithic architect and thereby connect back to our prehistoric ancestors. To what did they aspire?

As we enter a new millennium, Stonehenge's sixth, the apparently disparate subjects of archaeology, astronomy, metrology, sacred geometry, and even shamanism are slowly converging to reveal a holistic *megalithic science*.

Once part of an impressively large collection of stone circles throughout northwestern Europe, Stonehenge, with its raised circle of lintels yet differs from all the rest. Unique, and having survived five millennia and several cultural changes, Stonehenge is a Stone Age cathedral, the centerpiece of a once wealthy and evidently learned tribal community. Their magnificent legacy of stone beckons us to read its message.

St. Dogmaels, A.D. 2001

3

DIGGING IN THE DARK
the rediscovery of Stonehenge

Ever since the end of the Dark Ages, descriptions and illustrations of Stonehenge have been interwoven with the cultural fantasies of the time. So remote is the culture that originally built the monument that we should not be surprised at this. King James I's architect, Inigo Jones, added a sixth trilithon to link Stonehenge to Roman styles (*see page 51*), while Lucas de Herre's charming yet naive sketch (*see half title page*) is the first known sketch, drawn "on the spot" in 1569.

The bizarre and inaccurate engraving shown opposite is from William Campden's *Britannia* of 1605 and, for the first time, placed Stonehenge in front of a wider public. The Age of the Antiquarian dawned around 1650 with John Aubrey, and later William Stukeley, and Stonehenge became temple plus druids. Exit Roman and Greek influences and enter rude British.

Plundering of this and other ancient sites followed. A notorious duo, Colt-Hoare and Cunningham, practiced "reverse alchemy," replacing struck gold found in nearby burial mounds with lead tokens. In those days, archaeology was undertaken with pick axe and shovel, and much irrevocable damage was done and invaluable evidence irretrievably lost.

During the past century Colonel Hawley, Sir Matthew Flinders-Petrie, Sir Norman Lockyer, and professors Atkinson, Hawkins, and Thom each pioneered more scientific approaches to understanding Stonehenge. Despite these endeavors, many mysteries still remain within those "immemorial gray stones."

A The Stones call'd Corfstones, 12 Tonn Weight
  24 foot high, 7 broad, and 16 round
B The Stones call'd Coronetts, of 5 or 7 Tonn
C The place where Mens bones are dug up.

J. Kip S.

5

THE STONEHENGE LANDSCAPE
the remains on the plain

Stonehenge forms the centerpiece of a rich heritage, the remains of the so-called Wessex Culture, centered on Salisbury Plain. Within a few miles of the monument, the traveler may discover various types of *barrows*, or mounds, two unexplained *cursusses* (long rectangular swaths of land enclosed by embanked sides), Woodhenge (*see page 32*), many single standing stones, an 1,800-foot-long embanked avenue leading from Stonehenge, and a number of large postholes.

The impressive Stonehenge cursus is over two miles long and averages 420 feet in width, enclosing over 100 acres of land. It has variously been described as a UFO runway, a tornado strip, or a jousting arena. It was probably none of these, although one wonders why anyone might have wanted to construct such a strange alignment, especially so near to Stonehenge itself. Stukeley's 1740 engraving of the cursus is shown at the bottom of page 7.

Stonehenge also appears curiously and not ideally sited on sloping ground. Because of this, the perfectly level ring of elevated lintels required their massive supporting stones to be of varying height. The bulk of these stones, the so-called *Sarsen Stones*, some weighing 50 tons, had to be transported over 20 miles from their "quarry," a stone-littered valley on Fyfield Down near Avebury. The smaller bluestones came from Wales—over 150 miles away. This eloquently informs us that the architects chose the location of the site with great forethought.

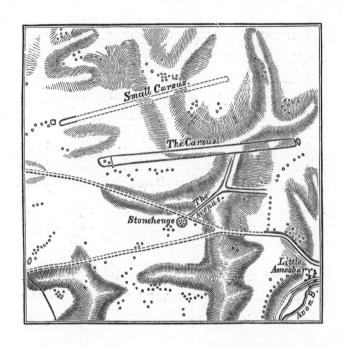

TRAVELS TO THE OTHERWORLD
a culture of life after death

The Stonehenge landscape includes many examples of what are known as barrows *(opposite)*. Many of these contained buried or cremated remains. The artifacts interred alongside the dead have provided archaeologists with much information about social patterns within the Wessex Culture. The fetal position of many of the skeletons suggests a rebirth from within Mother Earth. Many burial chambers throughout the entire megalithic culture are aligned to the midwinter sunrise or sunset, supporting such a theory, the symbolism being that, at the shortest days of midwinter, the "death" of the Sun thereafter leads to its resurrection, a daily increase in light, strength, and noonday height.

A recent excavation at Stonehenge unearthed the skeleton of an archer, with arrowheads still lodged in his vertebrae. Ritual sacrifice, execution, or murder? We will never know.

LONG BARROW

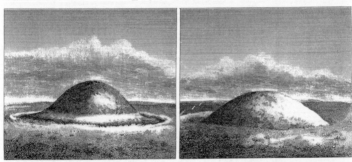

BELL BARROW   BOWL BARROW

DRUID BARROW

STONEHENGE CULTURE
artifacts from the past

What little we know about the people who built Stonehenge has traditionally come from archaeology. Accurate radiocarbon dating techniques have greatly assisted this process. Local museums in Salisbury and Devizes display wonderful treasures taken from the earth here. Fine gold artifacts, polished maces, riveted hilts, flint arrowheads, and elegant pottery contrast with crude stone maul hammers, arthritic bones, and low life-expectancy.

Polished mace and axe heads (*below*) date from 2500 B.C. and are often made from semiprecious stones. Fine, flat-bottomed beaker folk pottery (circa 2300 B.C.), finely chiseled arrowheads, and an exquisitely decorated ceremonial bronze axe head from 2000 B.C. (*all illustrated opposite*) reveal a culture the functional priorities of which were matched by artistic expertise. These people were not savages.

It is worthwhile imagining how such people could equip, feed, and organize the laborers who undertook Dr. Gerald Hawkins's estimated twelve million man-hours needed to construct Stonehenge, their finest artifact.

BARROWLOADS OF GOLD
a ninefold astronomical lozenge

At the Bush Barrow, an early Bronze Age site just south of Stonehenge, Stukeley found nothing, while Cunningham, in 1808, plundered his finest treasure—the so-called Bush Barrow *lozenge*.

Lying over the breast of a tall man, this exquisite artifact, made from beaten gold, was once mounted on a wooden plate, and measures 7 inches in length (*opposite*). Bronze rivets mixed with wood and thin strips of bronze were interred nearby. The lozenge may today be viewed at the Devizes Museum.

The internal angles of the lozenge are 80° and 100°, this reflecting a strong ninefold geometry to support the nine triangles along each side and the central diamond of nine smaller diamonds. Uniquely, at the latitude of Stonehenge, the extreme range of sunrises and sunsets occurs over an 80° span of the horizon; those of the Moon over 100° (*opposite, bottom right and left*). This has led some researchers to suggest that the lozenge was a sighting device and the tall man an astronomer-priest. But quite apart from any possible astronomical significance, the lozenge supplies firm evidence of advanced craft skills and a refined knowledge of geometry.

The man was also buried with two metal daggers, a bronze axe, a lance head, a second smaller gold lozenge, a gold belt hook, a stone mace head and decorated bone ornaments. In fact, not at all the normal gear of a modern astronomer!

ASTRONOMY AND GEOMETRY
a prehistoric culture of circle builders

In 1973 Alexander Thom undertook the first accurate survey of Stonehenge (*see half title page*). Previously having surveyed over five hundred stone circles, he had established that the builders used a unit of length of 2.72 feet (0.829m), which he called the *megalithic yard*. Stonehenge further confirmed this unit.

A third of Thom's surveyed stone circles were actually not circles at all, and their geometry derives from Pythagorean triangles, often in whole numbers of megalithic yards. Some examples are shown here; note how often the key points are marked by a stone. Some "circles," such as Castle Rigg, have their geometry aligned to key astronomical rising and setting positions of Sun, Moon, and stars, as does Stonehenge. Horizon landscape features were often skillfully incorporated. Ancient astronomers were using Pythagorean geometry with a rope-and-peg technology two thousand years before Pythagoras was born!

Recently a Type I Egg was discovered at Nabta, in the Sudan. It has been dated at 4500 B.C., the earliest known example of its type, and sited well away from the previously held boundaries of megalithic circle builders.

× TYPE I EGG ×

Druid Temple, Inverness
forming triangle 3:4:5
All dimensions in Megalithic Y.

● Upright stones
○ Fallen stones

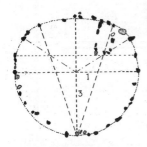

× TYPE "A" FLATTENED CIRCLE ×

CASTLE RIGG, KESWICK
forming triangle 1:3:√10
Diameter 40 MY

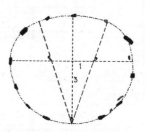

× TYPE "B" FLATTENED CIRCLE ×

Barbrook, Derbyshire
forming triangle 1:3:√10
(in units of 3 MY)

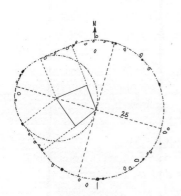

× TYPE II EGG ×

Borrowstone Rigg
forming triangle ∼ 3:4:5
Diameter 50 MY

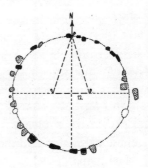

× ELLIPSE ×

Daviot "B"
forming triangle 12:35:37
(in units of quarter MY)

15

THE FIRST STONEHENGE
an implosion over 1,500 years

Stonehenge's concentric circles of stones and postholes evolved inward with time—the very opposite of a raindrop falling on water. This implosion evolved over fifteen hundred years.

The circular outer ditch and bank, once six feet high, is dated to around 3150 B.C. (*opposite, top*). The axis entrance, flanked by the then upright "slaughter stone" and a long-gone companion stone, was filled with many experimental posts, apparently to monitor the most northerly moonrises each month (*opposite, center*), particularly the extreme midwinter full moonrise that only occurs every eighteen years and seven months.

The entrance was later widened and the angle changed to that of the midsummer sunrise (*opposite, bottom*). The *Heel Stone*, "moated" within a small circular ditch marked the start of an eighteen-hundred-foot-long avenue, as shown on the extreme right of the top illustration opposite. Stonehenge, predominantly a lunar observatory in its early phases, apparently became more a solar observatory as it evolved, although we shall discover convincing evidence for soli-lunar observation, in the form of eclipse prediction and the establishment of an accurate calendar.

The name "Heel Stone" perhaps derives from the Welsh or Greek word for Sun, *haul* and *helios* respectively. Its other popular name, "Friar's Heel," is thought to refer to an indentation on the stone that resembles a heel print. However, *ffriw yr haul* is phonetically almost identical, being the Old Welsh for "appearance of the Sun."

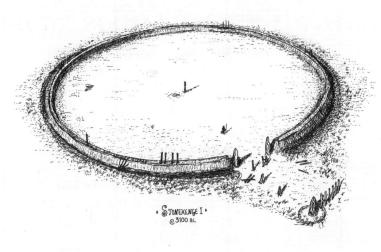

· STONEHENGE I ·
@ 3100 BC.

MOST NORTHERLY MOONRISE

MIDSUMMER SUNRISE

AUBREY HOLES AND STATION STONES
a wooden henge and a 5:12 rectangle

Around 3000 B.C., the circle of 56 Aubrey holes was dug, some think to provide sockets to house large posts supporting a level wooden henge platform long since rotted away (*opposite, top*). Three centuries later, four *Station Stones* were placed around the perimeter, defining the corners of an accurate 5:12 rectangle. This sets the *Aubrey Circle* diameter at 13 of the same units, each of 8 megalithic yards, totalling 104 MY (13 x 8) or 283 feet. This discovery confirmed the use of the megalithic yard by the builders to a skeptical archaeological establishment.

Just two stubs remain today of the four Station Stones. The two missing stones, perhaps 14 feet high, were sited on small mounds with surrounding ditches (*opposite, lower left*).

A central stone henge structure existed around this time, built from spotted dolerite bluestones, brought 135 miles as the crow flies. Several bluestones remaining on the site are curved, and possessed mortise holes. Some are tongued and grooved (*stone 68 opposite, lower right*). Perhaps 38 pairs of bluestones were used to complete a 90-foot-diameter circle of *trilithons*, apparently never completed, although the much disturbed central part of Stonehenge makes conclusive proof hard to attain. Maybe this first henge was imported complete from Wales, and some stones were lost en route?

The word *trilithon* derives from the Greek, "three stone," and refers to two upright stones supporting a third *lintel* above.

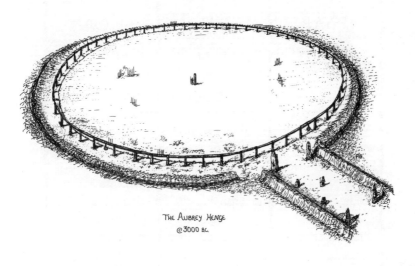

THE AUBREY HENGE
@ 3000 B.C.

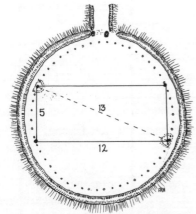

THE STATION STONE RECTANGLE © 2700 B.C.
~ UNITS = 8 MY ~

~ GROOVED BLUESTONE ~

19

SARSENS AND TRILITHONS
prehistoric monsters from a neolithic past

Around 2600 B.C. the famous *Sarsen Circle* was constructed, with its unique level circle of raised Sarsen Stone lintels, together with the five massive inner trilithons, of which three stand today. As the trilithon stones do not fit through the gaps in the Sarsen Circle, one must assume that these beasts were erected first. The Sarsens were brought from Fyfield Down, seventeen miles directly to the north of Stonehenge. The name *Sarsen* has been assumed to derive from "saracen," meaning "foreign."

The Sarsen Circle was dressed on the stones' inner faces, and once supported a complete circle of thirty lintels about 15 feet above the ground. The trilithons were more finely dressed, yet curiously one of each pair of uprights was left rough. The five trilithons varied in height from 17 to 25 feet. The diameter of the Sarsen Circle through the centerline of the lintels is 100.8 feet. The trilithon "horseshoe" takes an elliptical shape 40 by 70 feet.

Sarsen is a sandstone several times harder than granite, and was dressed on site using sarsen mauls weighing up to 63 pounds. Over eighteen hundred of these have been excavated, many used as backfill after the upright stones had been placed into their positions.

Before this mammoth undertaking the earlier bluestone henge was dismantled and afterwards rearranged within the Sarsen Circle as an inner circle of fifty-nine or sixty stones, 75 feet in diameter, together with a 39-foot horseshoe of nineteen slender examples, each stone standing about 7 feet high. Finally, the dressed 13-foot-high *altar stone* completed the edifice (*see page 47*).

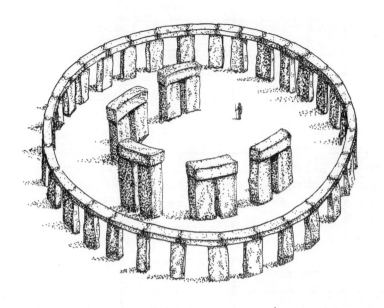

SARSEN CIRCLE

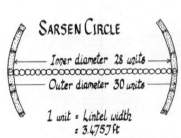

― Inner diameter 28 units ―

― Outer diameter 30 units ―

1 unit = Lintel width
= 3.4757 ft

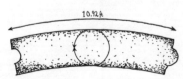

10.92 ft

SARSEN CIRCLE OUTER DIAMETER = 104.3ft

OUTER CIRCUMFERENCE = 327.6ft

INNER DIAMETER = 97.32ft

LINTEL LENGTH = 10.92 ft ($\frac{327.6}{30}$)

LINTEL WIDTH = 3.475 ft ($\frac{10.92}{\pi}$)

= LINTEL LENGTH $/\pi$

JEWISH SACRED ROD = 3.4757 ft

3.4757485ft = $\frac{\text{POLAR RADIUS}}{6,000,000}$

(after John Michell)

WOODWORK IN STONE
how to join up megaliths

The perfectly level circle of thirty curved Sarsen lintels was erected around the top of thirty supporting Sarsen uprights. In order to fix these securely, some thirteen feet above the ground they were locked together like pieces of a jigsaw puzzle, using tongues and grooves. In addition, each upright was dressed with two tenons that mated with corresponding mortises on the lintels (*below*). The visitor may observe the tenons on many Sarsen uprights where the lintels have fallen (*see for example stones 56 and 60 opposite, bottom*). These jointing techniques derive from the wood joiner's craft.

The mighty trilithon uprights carried a large single tenon, and their lintels were duly mortised. The tallest stone (*56*) still sports its tenon, like a boy's school cap thrown up as a prank, while its curiously double-mortised lintel has fallen.

The pictures opposite are from Barclay's *Stonehenge*, 1895 (*see page 47 for the full stone numbering classification*).

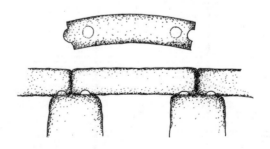

2000 B.C.—an idealized view from the south showing the half-width Sarsen

A.D. 1900—Stonehenge before restoration showing a silhouetted bluestone (62)

A.D. 1900—view from the south showing the once perilously leaning trilithon upright (56)

23

ERECTING THE STONES
the fine art of levitating lintels

Fetching fifty-ton Sarsen Stones from Fyfield Down and four- or five-ton bluestones from the Preseli Mountains in Wales must have demanded a good working technology of ropes and levers, rollers and cradles. And plenty of spare time!

The large stones were dressed on site and rolled or dragged to a waiting hole socket. A cranelike structure was probably used to pull them up to the vertical. Perhaps the "Y" and "Z" holes, shown in the plan on page 29, held the props for this perilous process—for no stones were ever placed in them.

It is assumed, without a shred of evidence, that the lintels were raised by progressively adding to the height of a wooden cradle while levering up the lintel. Presumably the lintel was then perilously slid across to meet the awaiting tenons in the Sarsen uprights. Do not try this at home! Is it unfeasible to suppose that an earth or timber ramp may have been used? Levitation? Any other ideas?

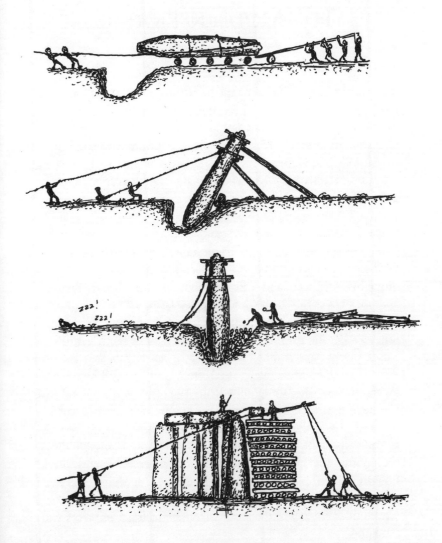

zzz!

zzz!

25

THE MODERN PICTURE
our semiruinous legacy

The construction of Stonehenge began around 3150 B.C. and was over by about 1500 B.C. Thereafter, it fell victim to the vagaries of the British climate and lay at the mercy of several cultural changes. As late as 1917 the authorities submitted an application to demolish Stonehenge as "a dangerous hazard to low-flying aircraft"! Remarkably, it has survived—after a fashion. The site is now surrounded by security fences, a parking lot, and a souvenir shop—temples to a different god.

Many visitors have carved graffiti on the stones, which has conferred on them an ersatz immortality. Mycean daggers may be discerned (*opposite, top*). The relentless erosion of the Sarsen Stone by wind, rain, and frost has produced some bizarre gnarling and pockmarks in which some folks see faces, totem animals, and even goddesses. In 1797 trilithon four fell, shaking the ground miles away. During the last night of the nineteenth century, a Sarsen upright and its lintel fell (*stones 22 and 122 on the plan, page 47*). In 1958, these were re-erected, and the following year several more stones straightened. In 1963, stone 23, a lintel that had been disturbed by the earlier restoration, fell and was quickly restored. Over the ages, some fallen stones have disappeared off-site, perhaps to be broken up and used in less interesting buildings.

Opposite is a French reproduction of an engraving by David Loggan from the mid-seventeenth century. It shows the huge trilithon upright, stone 56, leaning perilously. The restoration work pulled it back to the vertical, but its mate lies in pieces with the lintel.

26

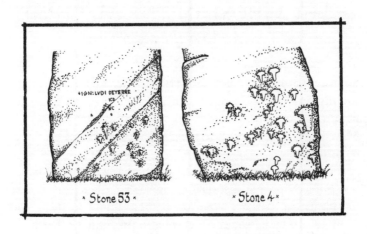

* Stone 53 *   * Stone 4 *

Vûe de STONE-HENGE du Côté d'Occident.

THE GHOST IN THE MACHINE
reading the stones

So just what have we got here on Salisbury Plain? Through all the mystery and speculation is it possible to separate fact from fiction, theory from hard-won observation and proof? And how do we begin to understand what Stonehenge was about, to read the "service manual" for the monument?

Perhaps the best one can do is to recognize that Stonehenge was built by people identical to ourselves, albeit very different in culture yet perhaps superior in their ability to think about some fundamental issues concerning human life on Earth.

In addition, the stones did not arrive or become placed by magic. The site was prepared, surveyed, measured, and marked out by people like us. Stones were transported, men and animals fed, and equipment brought in and maintained. This was a colossal project of high importance to these people, and it must be true that someone was the architect of the various phases and knew precisely what he or she was undertaking.

Early in 1963, Mr. C. A. Newham shed some light on our darkness. Newham discovered the remarkable link between solar and lunar astronomy (*opposite*) and the geometry of the Station Stones. This revelation was taken further by a noted American professor of astronomy, Dr. Gerald Hawkins, who found other significant alignments. In 1965 he published a best-selling book, *Stonehenge Decoded*, which was scathingly attacked by many archaeologists. The new discipline of *archaeoastronomy* had arrived.

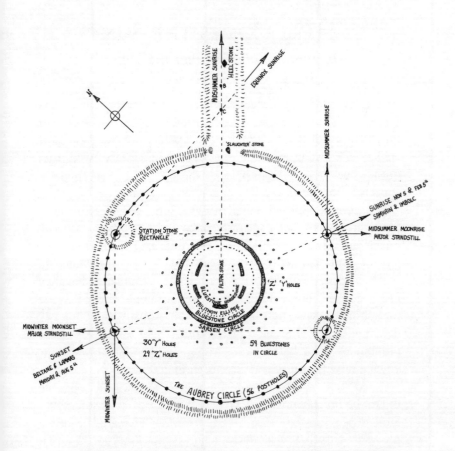

In March 1963 Mr. C. A. Newham wrote an article for the Yorkshire
Post that revealed the solar and lunar alignments of the Station Stone
rectangle (above). These alignments apply only at the latitude of
Stonehenge; elsewhere the rectangle would become a parallelogram. The
geometry is entirely octagonal (see page 49).

HERE COMES THE SUN
the famous midsummer alignment

At the latitude of Stonehenge, the annual range of sunrises and sunsets each sweep angles of 40° on either side of an east-west line. The Bush Barrow lozenge (*see page 13*) displays these same angles. The midsummer sunrise, shown opposite viewed from outside the Sarsen Circle through the towering giant trilithon, appears from a point on the horizon along the avenue.

The commonly held belief that the sun rises over the Heel Stone at midsummer is actually incorrect. All those beautiful images are a trick or fabrication, taken off axis (*see opposite, top*). Yet the Sun did actually rise from the axis of the avenue in Neolithic times; since then the Earth's angle of tilt has reduced by half a degree. Stonehenge was indeed a temple aligned to the midsummer sunrise, and thereby to the seasonal year of 365.242 days, but the Heel Stone is placed to the right of the axis of the monument. The "Heel Stone rising" is therefore more convincing now than it would have been in 2500 B.C.

In addition, the midwinter sunset lies almost exactly opposite the midsummer sunrise and, viewed from the avenue, shines into Stonehenge from the southwest (*see pages 41 and 43*). As a processional walkway the Stonehenge avenue (*see page 55*) is far more appropriate to midwinter than to midsummer rituals. Anthropologist Dr. Lionel Sims has recently noted that the avenue is not level and that a walk along it at the midwinter solstice sunset would enable the celebrants to observe two sunsets before entering the enclosure at the center of Stonehenge.

WOODHENGE
another midsummer alignment

Just down the road, two miles to the northeast of Stonehenge, lies Woodhenge, a most interesting Neolithic site. Dating from 2000 B.C., archaeologists think it may have been a roofed building. Whatever Woodhenge once was, like Stonehenge it was built with its axis accurately aligned to the midsummer sunrise. The cursus (*see page* 7) points to the site.

The complex arrangement of postholes holds an interesting geometry, for Woodhenge is six concentric ellipsoids in plan, having perimeters of 40, 60, 80, 100, 140, and 160 megalithic yards, the whole design based on the 12:35:37 Pythagorean right triangle of half MY units—and one wonders why.

Many megalithic sites have their entrances aligned to a solstice sunrise or sunset. The most famous are Newgrange in Ireland, Bryn Celli-Ddu on Anglesey, Maes Howe in the Orkneys and, of course, Stonehenge. These are ritual alignments, of low resolution accuracy, connecting man with the skies and to the seasonal flow of time. Our Neolithic forebears were evidently very interested in the seasonal variations in the rising and setting positions of the Sun and Moon.

Some megalithic sites align to key astronomical points on a far distant horizon that are accurate to a sixtieth of a degree. Many mark the 18.62 year lunar cycle, particularly those sites thought to have been used to detect the tiny seventh of a degree up and down the 173 day "wobble" of the Moon's orbit, vital for predicting eclipses. The best example is Temple Wood, Argyllshire.

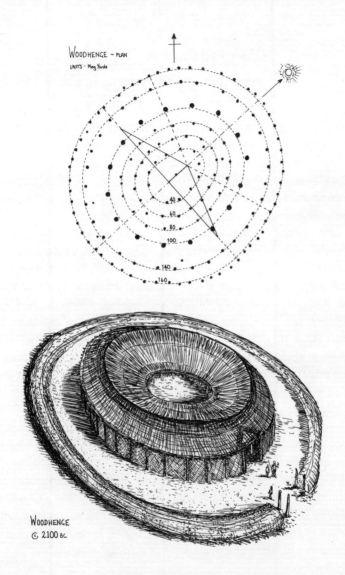

WOODHENGE ~ PLAN

UNITS : Meg Yards

40
60
80
100
140
160

WOODHENGE
ⓒ 2100 B.C.

CALENDAR CAPERS
the reasons for the seasons

At Stonehenge one repeatedly finds the numbers of the solar year and lunar month in the numbers of stones and their dimensional spacing. In the diagram on page 29, we found that uniquely at the latitude of Stonehenge a 5:12 rectangle defines all eight solar festivals still celebrated in our present culture. In addition, it aligns with the extreme standstill positions of the Moon.

The 56-hole Aubrey Circle suggests the ancient calendar of 13 months of 28 days—a 364 day year. The 30 upright stones of the Sarsen Circle suggest the Egyptian calendar of 12 months of 30 days—totaling 360 days. More crucially, 29 of the uprights were full width and one was deliberately made half-width (*see page 47, stone 11, and top illustration, page 23, the smaller stone fifth from the left*). Was this an attempt to represent in stone the $29\frac{1}{2}$ day lunation cycle (the time between two full moons)? Twice 29.5 makes 59, the number of "Y" and "Z" holes and also the number of stones in the bluestone circle.

The bluestone horseshoe once contained 19 stones. Why? In 19 years there are exactly 235 lunations—a near perfect repeat cycle of the Sun and Moon, called the *Metonic cycle*. Other close repeat cycles occur after 3, 5, and 8 years.

Divide 235 by 19 and you get $12\frac{7}{19}$, the number of lunations (full moons) in one year. Seven nineteenths is 0.368. The mean Sarsen Circle diameter is 3 x 12.368 MY (100.9 feet) and the ratio between the Aubrey Circle diameter and Sarsen Circle outer diameter is 7/19 (*opposite, bottom*). A curious coincidence?

SOLAR YEAR 365.242 days
LUNAR MONTH 29.53059 days (LUNATION)
MONTHS IN YEAR 12.368 (12⁷⁄₁₉)

ONE MEGALITHIC YARD 2.72 ft	
1 FOOT	1 ROYAL CUBIT 1.72 ft

ONE LUNAR MONTH 29.531 days	
7⁄19 LUNAR MONTHS	12⁄19 LUNAR MONTHS

12 LUNAR MONTHS	SOLAR YEAR	13 LUNAR MONTHS
354.367 days	365.242 days	383.898 days

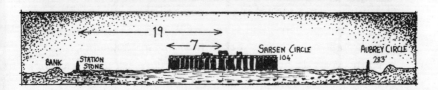

ALTERNATIVE STONEHENGE
the loony fringe of dotty archaeology

Stonehenge has always attracted speculation, which reached a climactic peak in the 1960s. Unfortunately, at this time the discovery that the entire chronology of the Neolithic and Bronze Age periods was hopelessly in error threw archaeologists into ferment, and they closed ranks over this invasion of their territory. As a result, much valid research in megalithic geometry, astronomy, and metrology (the units of length used by the builders) was castigated, mocked, or ignored. Any nonarchaeologist was automatically assumed, in Professor Atkinson's immortal phrase, to belong to the "loony fringe of dotty archaeology."

In 1965 Dr. Hawkins published *Stonehenge Decoded*; Atkinson called it "Moonshine over Stonehenge." In 1967 Professor Thom's seminal *Megalithic Sites in Britain* was described as "putting a time bomb under archaeology." Finally, in 1969 John Michell's revelatory and best-selling *The View over Atlantis* presented a picture of ancient Britain that no archaeologist could stomach. Here was convincing evidence of huge straight alignments running tens, sometimes hundreds of miles over Britain. The legends, myths, sacred sites, and even the town names indicated a folk memory and a landscape etched with patterns from an ancient "spiritual engineering" that once covered the entire land. Lea lines, sacred geometry, and astronomical aligments became a fad, reviving other ancient arts such as dowsing and feng-shui.

Thirty years later, these things are more accepted by the ordinary citizen, while most archaeologists remain skeptical.

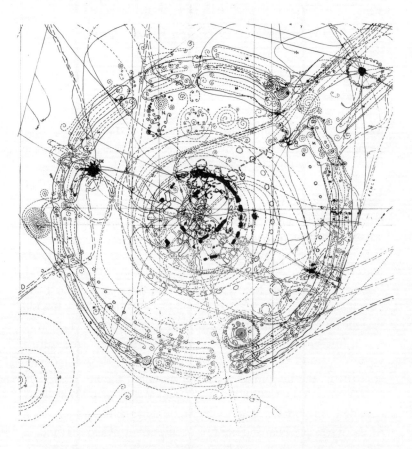

In 1948 Guy Underwood dowsed around Stonehenge, producing the above schematic of the "earth energies" he sensed. He also, for the first time, correctly dated the monument at 2650 B.C. His book Pattern of the Past helped to fuel a revival in the ancient art of dowsing.

THE LUNATION TRIANGLE
the marriage of the Sun and Moon

A soli–lunar calendar must, in advance, correctly place the dates of full and new moons within the year. There are 12.368 lunations (full moons) in one solar year. One technique for finding this number is both simple and accurate, and Stonehenge fully supports its use in the Station Stone rectangle. A 5:12 rectangle has a diagonal of 13. The resulting 5:12:13 Pythagorean triangle can readily enable a new hypotenuse of length 12.368 units to be constructed (*opposite, top*). The 153 fishes caught in the disciples' net in St. John, Chapter XXI, suggests arcane knowledge of the lunation triangle, as 153 is 12.369^2.

The lunation triangle shown opposite connects Stonehenge with the bluestone site and makes a right angle at Lundy Island. Loony fringe? Well, Lundy's Old Welsh name was Ynys Elen, "the island of the elbow, or right angle." In Welsh myth, the old straight tracks were under the protection of Elen, the goddess of sunset (the west). The British princess Helen, who came from a western island, presumed to be Angle-sea, was said to have constructed the long straight roads throughout the kingdom.

This large triangle, 2,500 times larger than the Station Stone rectangle, provides a reason why Stonehenge is located where it is, and why the bluestone site was so important. Caldey Island, at the 3:2 point, hosts the earliest surviving Celtic Christian church.

Astonishingly, the extension of the line connecting the bluestone site to Stonehenge eventually passes through the Giza Pyramid complex in Egypt, a weird but incontestable fact.

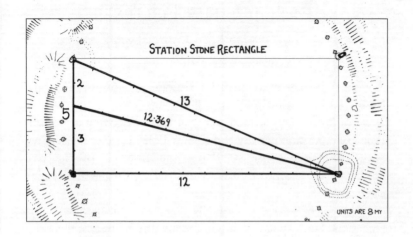

STATION STONE RECTANGLE

2

5

3

13

12·369

12

UNITS ARE 8 MY

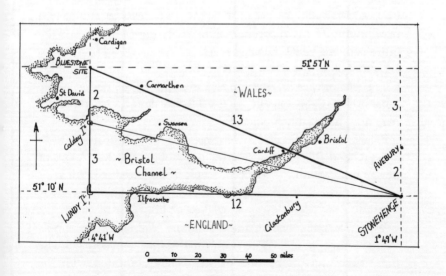

· Cardigan

BLUESTONE SITE

51° 57'N

· Carmarthen

~WALES~

St David

2

Caldey I.

3

· Swansea

~ Bristol
Channel ~

Cardiff ·

· Bristol

AVEBURY ·

3

2

LUNDY I.

· Ilfracombe

12

51° 10'N

13

Glastonbury ·

STONEHENGE

~ENGLAND~

4° 41'W

1° 49'W

0   10   20   30   40   50 miles

39

PREDICTING ECLIPSES
who nodes how holds power

Anyone who has tried to make a model of how the Sun and Moon move around the sky will end up, most simply, with a circle of 28 markers around a central Earth. Moving a "Moon-Pole" one position per day and a "Sun-Pole" once every 13 days, both counterclockwise, replicates the motions of the two luminaries around the Zodiac, and thereby provides an accurate calendar.

Twice every year, for about 34 days, any full or new moon crosses the Sun's apparent path in the sky (the ecliptic) and eclipses result. These two *eclipse seasons*, which are 173 days apart, move backward around the calendar taking 18.6 years to complete a revolution. The two precise points where the Moon crosses the Sun's path are called the *lunar nodes*.

By doubling the 28 markers to 56, as found in the Aubrey Circle (*shown opposite*), we can also incorporate the period of the lunar nodes. Conveniently, 18.6 x 3 is also almost 56, and eclipses may now be reliably predicted.

Professor Sir Fred Hoyle was the first astronomer to comprehend this practical use for the Aubrey Circle. A full or new moon within the shaded "eclipse zone" predicts a lunar or solar eclipse. A lunar eclipse will always be visible at a given location if the Moon rises within the half hour before sunset.

Why not build one of these at home, following the simple instructions opposite? The nodal markers are moved clockwise three times a year, by one marker. They coincided with the midsummer/midwinter axis, on October 23, 2001.

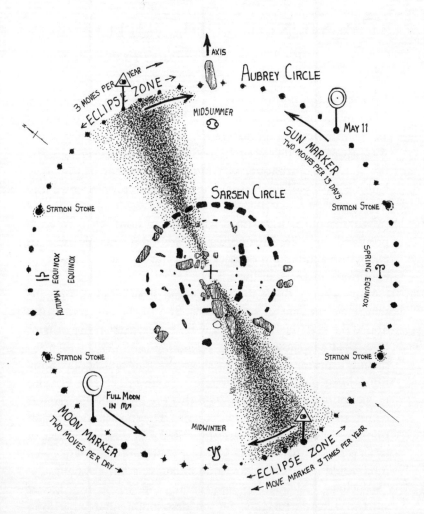

AXIS

3 MOVES PER YEAR

ECLIPSE ZONE

MIDSUMMER

AUBREY CIRCLE

SUN MARKER
TWO MOVES PER 13 DAYS

MAY 11

SARSEN CIRCLE

STATION STONE

STATION STONE

AUTUMN EQUINOX
EQUINOX

SPRING EQUINOX

STATION STONE

STATION STONE

FULL MOON IN ♏

MOON MARKER
TWO MOVES PER DAY

MIDWINTER

♑

ECLIPSE ZONE
MOVE MARKER 3 TIMES PER YEAR

STONEHENGE COMPLETE
not just a load of old lintels

Ever since the midsummer axis (*opposite*) was first spotted by William Stukeley, it has been clear that there is an astronomical and geometrical component to the monument. This alignment was first measured accurately by Sir Norman Lockyer in 1901, but the lunar astronomy was missed for another half century because our culture had previously failed to recognize the importance of the Moon within megalithic culture.

As archaeologists Dr. Euan MacKie and Lord Renfrew have proposed, an elite astronomer-priesthood seemingly able to extinguish a full moon or blacken out the Sun would have held enormous power over the tribe.

Many visitors think that the central stone construction, to which we turn next, is all there is to Stonehenge, and hardly notice the concrete filled Aubrey holes as they step over them. But, as Hoyle showed, these are numerically perfect for predicting eclipses, and can also show the Sun and Moon positions, lunar phase, and the state of the sea tides. The Greeks, in the fourth century B.C., taught that the number fifty-six was connected with eclipses and dragons. The lunar nodes, which rule when eclipses occur, are still called *caput draconis* and *caput cauda* (dragon's head and tail) in many astronomy books.

It would not affect the monument one bit to have the "Stonehenge calendar" up and running today as an educational aid for visitors. Imagine the job description—but what long hours!

ROLLING STONES
the art of long-distance megalith moving

The huge Sarsen Stones were moved over 20 miles from Fyfield Down, next to Avebury (*see page 52*). Modern attempts to re-create the journey have shown just how hard this must have been. In 1923, the smaller bluestones, weighing up to five tons, were shown by Dr. H. H. Thomas to have originated from a small area of the Preseli Mountains in modern Pembrokeshire, about 135 miles from Stonehenge. How they were moved still remains conjectural. A recent attempt to replicate this journey failed utterly, the bluestone sinking in Milford Harbour after several other dangerous mishaps.

Some people think the bluestones arrived at Stonehenge by glacial action. However, the large central altar stone (*opposite, top*) is made of a sparkly green micaceous sandstone found adjacent to the Haven, never glaciated. It is more likely that these stones were hauled to Milford Haven, then rafted, either to the Bristol Avon, thence to Stonehenge, or around the Devon and Cornwall coastline to Hengistbury, a thriving prehistoric port on the Hampshire Avon (*opposite, bottom*). The bluestones were evidently of crucial importance to the project.

The latitudes from which the bluestone and the Sarsen Stones were taken are precisely one seventh of 364 and 360 respectively. These numbers formed the year in ancient calendars, for 13-month and 12-month years respectively. Seven-fold geometry is found to link the Aubrey Circle with the Sarsen Circle (*see page 49*).

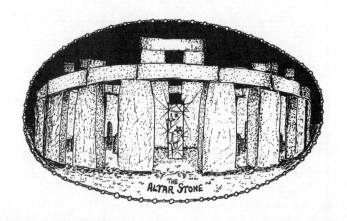

THE
ALTAR STONE

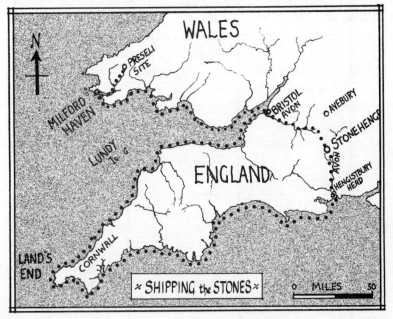

N

WALES

PRESELI
SITE

MILFORD
HAVEN

LUNDY
Is.

BRISTOL
AVON

AVEBURY

STONEHENGE

AVON

HENGISTBURY
HEAD

ENGLAND

LAND'S
END

CORNWALL

~ SHIPPING the STONES ~

0   MILES   50

THE MIDDLE GROUND
the stones at the center

With nearly one million visitors a year, Stonehenge is under increasing threat from the sheer numbers of people who wish to wander inside the world's most visited megalithic sacred site. To walk inside the central area of the monument today requires that a visitor apply well in advance for special access from the custodians, English Heritage.

The plan shown opposite, of the central area enclosed by the Sarsen Circle, is from Edgar Barclay's 1895 book *Stonehenge and its Earthworks*. Apart from the fact that the fallen trilithon (stones 57 and 58 and lintel 158) has since been re-erected, in 1958, this plan is very similar to the Stonehenge we see today. The concentric solid lines indicate the bluestone horseshoe, bluestone circle, and Sarsen Circle respectively.

Barclay's numbering system for the stones remains the standard classification to this day. Of particular interest is stone 11, the half-width Sarsen upright; stone 150, a bluestone with mortise holes; and stone 68, the grooved bluestone (*see page 19*).

Shown also is stone 156, the trilithon lintel curiously mortised on both sides, which has been presumed to be an error made by the builders. However, the symmetry of the curved lintel would have enabled it to have been placed above stones 156 and 157 either away around. Might we speculate that once there was an additional construction above this highest platform at Stonehenge? Certainly, such a placing would have been entirely appropriate, although we are never likely to know what form it took, nor its purpose.

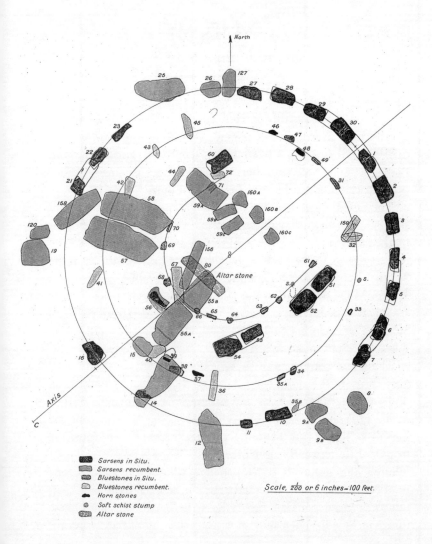

North

Axis

C

Altar stone

Sarsens in Situ.
Sarsens recumbent.
Bluestones in Situ.
Bluestones recumbent.
Horn stones
Soft schist stump
Altar stone

Scale, 200 or 6 inches=100 feet.

47

SACRED GEOMETRY
how to build a temple

The megalithic architects were researching into geometry. We have proposed that this linked the Stonehenge site with its astronomical functions, but it may have done much more than that. Repeated use of a fixed unit of length and fascination with Pythagorean whole number triangles suggests there was a geometrical intent and layout for the monument.

The essential geometry of Stonehenge invokes the numbers 7 and 8 in an elegant synthesis. If every eighth Aubrey hole is marked out and they are connected as shown opposite, the resulting 7-sided "star" correctly defines the mean diameter of the Sarsen Circle at 100.9 feet, which is 37.1 megalithic yards (or 3 x 12.368 MY). In addition the Aubrey Circle and Station Stones are precisely defined by an octagonal star suspended from the Heel Stone. The enclosing circle has exactly the same radius as the long side of the Station Stone rectangle, 96 MY (261 feet).

These two constructions show 7 and 8 combined. Multiplied they give 56, the number of Aubrey holes, the key number in understanding the calendar and eclipses. If we imagine Stonehenge to represent the Earth itself, and its axis to represent the Earth's axis, then the Station Stone rectangle also emulates the tropics of Cancer and Capricorn.

Surely the architects of Stonehenge were aware of the geometrical ratios, astronomy, and repeated lengths built into their temple? How could it otherwise have been built with these things included? Their temple was a repository of their wisdom.

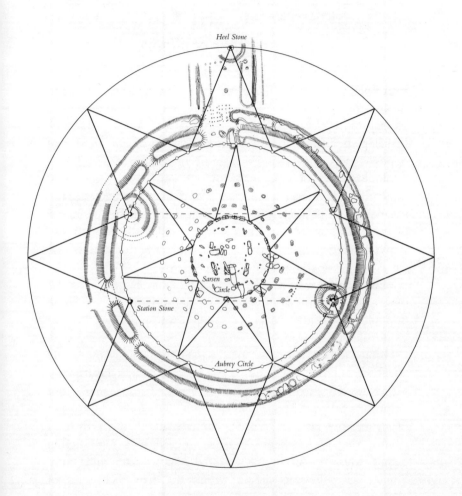

SURVEYING THE CIRCLE
three centuries of inquiry

Ever since Inigo Jones's hexagonal linking of the Sarsen Circle to the five trilithons (in 1655 the King's architect thought there were six [*opposite, top left*]) people have surveyed and interpreted Stonehenge, particularly the inner sanctum. Various designs are shown opposite, each attributed to their respective author.

John Michell's most elegant solution to squaring the circle using the Earth and Moon (*bottom center*) also defines two circles of the inner sanctum of Stonehenge. In a squared circle the perimeter of the square and circle are the same. Michell's diagram also shows a triangular solution that correctly sizes both the bluestone circle and horseshoe within the Sarsen Circle.

John Martineau's recent octagonal solution (*bottom right*) masterfully accounts for the width of the stones in the bluestone horseshoe. His other octagonal solution was shown on the previous page.

Throughout Stonehenge one discovers meticulous and subtle attention to detail. For example, the two Sarsen uprights flanking the midsummer axis (*see page 43*) are placed just a single foot farther apart than the rest. The half width Sarsen upright, the use of accurate measures and precise geometry, and the perfectly level circular ring of lintels are evidence indeed of a sophisticated people whose endeavor has endured into its sixth millenium. Stonehenge still bears ample witness to their high level of civilization. It was their temple, revealing their cosmology, and one wonders what else lies hidden within these ancient stones.

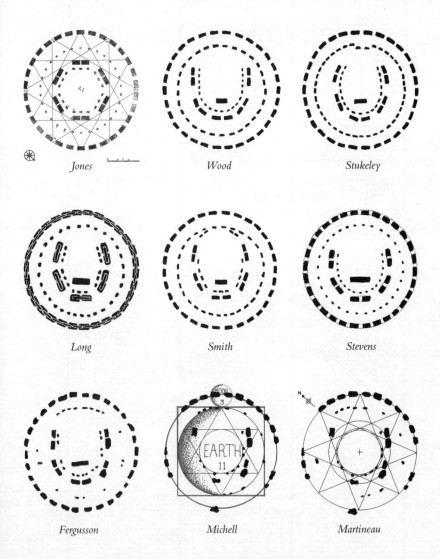

Jones

Wood

Stukeley

Long

Smith

Stevens

Fergusson

Michell

Martineau

51

Stonehenge Dwarfed
Avebury, the world's largest stone circle

The huge Sarsen Stone Circle at Avebury has a perimeter two-thirds of a mile around, using stones up to 60 tons in weight. Now ruinous, and once part of an immense neolithic complex centered on the source of the Stonehenge Sarsen Stones, Avebury lies 17 miles due north of its younger cousin. The center of the Avebury henge is located at a latitude precisely 360/7 degrees. Stukeley's famed "serpent" engraving of 1743 is shown below.

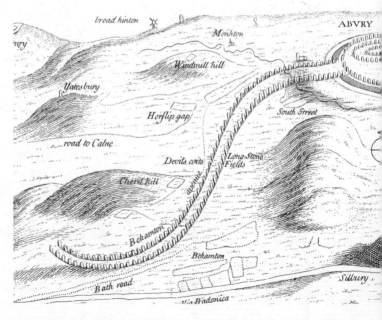

The main stone circle once consisted of 99 stones and fed two long stone avenues. Nearby one may still find Europe's largest artificial earthen mound, the magnificent Silbury Hill, several long barrows (*see page 55*), and a wonderfully intact Neolithic landscape.

Like Stonehenge, Avebury may also be used to provide a calendar. In eight years, the Sun, Moon and Venus repeat their cycles, within a day or two, after 99 lunations. The two internal circles, 340 feet in diameter, are both larger than Stonehenge. They once counted 27 and 29 stones, totalling 56 and strongly suggesting the two lunar monthly cycles of 27.3 and 29.5 days.

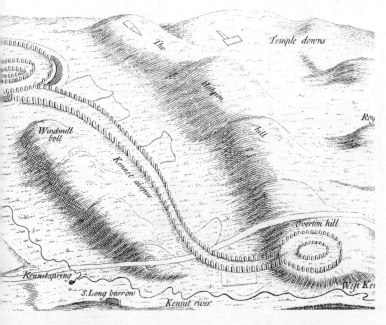

STAR CULTURE
high spirits in the night sky

Before Stonehenge and the start of Neolithic culture, the people of southern Britain built *long barrows*—multiple chambered burial mounds. Good examples include Belas Knap, Gloucestershire; Winterbourne Stoke, near Stonehenge; and West Kennet Avebury (*opposite*). These enigmatic structures, like giants' sleeping bags, were often aligned to important risings and settings of stars. The diagram below (*after Thom*) shows the setting points of major fixed stars on the western horizon in 2000 B.C.

Stars rise and set at a given location from the same places for hundreds of years, and alignments to these fixed places on the horizon would have indicated security at a time when the Sun and Moon's motions were perhaps not yet fully understood. Aerial photographs of the British landscape often reveal the remnants of long straight tracks, pre-Roman, extending for tens, sometimes hundreds of miles, often aligned to ancient star risings and settings. We may never glimpse the true picture of prehistoric Britain, before Stonehenge, when stars were the sky gods.

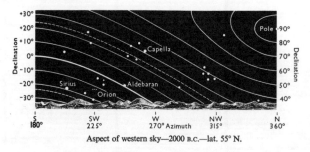

Aspect of western sky—2000 B.C.—lat. 55° N.

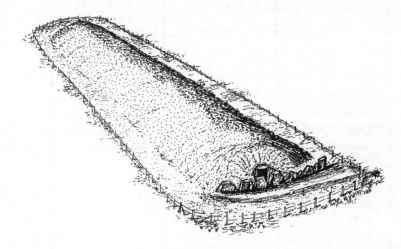

~ West Kennet Long Barrow ~

INSPIRATIONAL STONEHENGE
a source of wonder and amazement

Stonehenge may elude us, but it also inspires us. The monument taunts our smallness, yet celebrates our abilities. Our culture assumes superiority while those stones point to things we have forgotten, and they mock our hubris in so doing. We might humbly remember the words of the poet Drayton, who, in *Polyalbion*, wrote:

> *"Ill did those mighty men to trust thee with their story,*
> *Thou hast forgot their names, who raised thee for their glory."*

And to drive the point home, the American novelist Henry James wrote that,

> *"There is something in Stonehenge almost reassuring, and if you are disposed to think that life is rather a superficial matter, and that we soon get to the bottom of things, the immemorial gray pillars may serve to remind you of the enormous backdrop of time."*

Many poets and writers have dipped their pens into the dark ink of James's "immemorial gray pillars," and Stonehenge has also inspired many fine artists throughout history; Constable, Turner, Blake, and Henry Moore all worked with the monument, as did melodramatic lesser artists (*see opposite*).

Perhaps, like the black monolith in Arthur C. Clarke's *2001, A Space Odyssey*, Stonehenge enables a process of increased consciousness, most notably of the true rhythms of human life and the cycles of the Sun and Moon. We moderns have lost most of that, and need with some urgency to reclaim our long-lost legacy from the past, frozen in time and space at Stonehenge.

"It's true Edgar, the solstice was yesterday!"

Further Reading

Sun, Moon & Earth by Robin Heath (Walker & Company, 2001)
A Guide to the Stone Circles of Britain, Ireland & Brittany
by Aubrey Burl (Yale, 1996)
Stonehenge, Mysteries of the Stones and Landscape
by David Souden (English Heritage, 1997).
Sun, Moon & Stonehenge by Robin Heath (Bluestone Press, 1998)

Other books are mentioned in the text.

STONEHENGE, AS IT WAS AND AS IT IS.
THE ENCLOSURE OF THE ANCIENT MONUMENT.